Content warning:

This book contains themes of depression/mental illness, death, and drug abuse.

better places

(a collected collection of collections)

by:

ben st.john

one:
cotard's delusion
live forever
the days
anymore
colossus
nothingness face
less
bears
new normal
reaming
ungiven
nights
unexplained
as it was
only

two:
no heroes
invasion of the cousin
snatchers
a beautiful place somewhere
far away
born like it
equality in isolation
protest llc
imagine
the semi-physical world
target of the day
barker
high noon
friend's house
the following
moths
over (and over and over a-)

three:
attention attention
to the many who shared
their time with me
longer still
another week
strangelove
brothers don't say
mishmash
pov
mine, yours, and mine
the window by the sink
exes in oh
remember me

four:
hotel
maybe
missed
unf
noise
and this is now
pride
i was a teenage incel
walking
out in the open
gambler's fallacy
lad lard
what's next
witness
thirst
listen
'o brother
primal insecurity
town
30 years
plans

five:
ripple
following time
vu
downtime
after
the big harrumph
duty
us all
everything you've ever
wanted (and more)
like family
it's only life
i am
show me
always

book one
'another yesterday'

fuck it

the way this goes
we've been here, before

things have hit the bottom
beneath and below
in the basement of the cellar

the word i'm trying to find
hasn't been defined
for this experience

i find it ironic
in a world trapped indoors
we can't find a way out

our toys and things
air conditioned recliners
the perpetual television stream

the world of interior suffering
was merely just
years in the making

death and destruction

the way things go
we've been here before.

- *"cotard's
delusion "*

live forever

why?

what's the purpose of
another day of yesterday?

i find it meaningless
to trudge

i've been dying forever
why do it again?

- *"live
forever"*

the days, the days

playgrounds and video games
fast food after school
on tuesdays and thursdays

spongebob themed birthdays
at grandma's pool

cold orange pop

i had it good
better than most.

- *" the days "*

i don't have too long, now
to keep this going on
i don't have too much, now
to act like i can just
move on through the waves
i don't have much, now
to keep me where i need

if this is life as it is

simply, don't wait for me.

can't stop the tears
can't stop the time
can't stop the end
can't change my mind.

- *" anymore "*

sixteen, scaled
to save my love

the light led me there
the blood in my eyes

forbidden lands
never to return
the desert i came in
the forest i bypassed

this promise i was given

the only friend i had.

- *"colossus"*

nothingness face
i kiss everyday
and see everyday

what i tell them
nothing i couldn't
say about myself

cold, so empty
all the same

out to hurt me

out to kill me.

- *"nothingness
face"*

i'm okay
simple wishes
let me please
get through today

head carried on hand
i'm not too strong
to carry this
far longer,
anymore

and if i fall asleep
and never wake up
don't wake me
just, please
let me be.

- *" less "*

monday meetings downtown
dad used to take me

fruit punch buffalo blood

pinewood cars
i watched a movie
while he made it next door

friends young and new
just as we were.

- *"bears "*

you don't want knowledge
of things i want to do to me

i'm exhausted of
this way of thinking

against my will

just as it as

god knows this can't last
a cycle of exhaustion
from s to another s

as if i could.

- *" new normal "*

i have lived
far too long
eyes closed inside

walking by
oblivious
cannot

no return, praying for
a chance to just
sleep,
forever

in my head
in my room
in myself
in only dreams
in a delusion

i've burned far too long
i've hurt far too much
i've done far too much
please
i've done far too much.

- *" reaming "*

twenty years i've been
and for twenty years
borrowed time

and for another
twenty years

will be time i'll waste.

- " ungiven "

this side of the fire
on the fourth of july

warm, gooey s'mores
family conversation

singed fingertips
gripping a spark

that house they don't
live in anymore.

- *" nights "*

cannot tell why
cannot be changed
loved or remembered

i don't blame you
i wouldn't myself

i'm scraping by
making it to bed and
rolling out.

- *"unexplained "*

i was myself once
his ass was kicked in school

i miss the old days
but they were running out

spending a fickle youth
feeling like i'm so dead

from such a giving family
i never spend much time around.

- *" as it was "*

i've only gotten older
the end drawing close
things i can never
be

i'll never be.

- *" only "*

book two
'permanent fire'

nothing i know can save us
from inevitable demise
no heroes, no christs
no standout people like us
everything made to fall right down
debris to crush those below

nothing I know can save us
from our own oblivion
no wisdoms, no lessons
no friendly hands to grab
everyone's only dying quicker
any faith for change gone forever

all hope is lost
nothing's left to say, to change
it's not a matter now of
how much time there is
to make a difference
it's now just a matter of time
before all is left to waste

from our hands, from our mouths
no scapegoats to point at
it's always been our way
to seek those to blame
it's not a matter of 'who'
but a matter of 'who's not.'

- "no heroes "

climb that wall, men
the stairs can't hold us

an invasion
empty offices
we have them surrounded

more of us
we got them running

big boss man
gave the order

don't let them in
don't give 'em the chance

'real patriots'
as we call ourselves.

*- "invasion of
the cousin
snatchers "*

endless green sea

the village home here

limited slots for heaven

dream cottage
clothed in stone, moss, and age
and a 6 figure tag

median age:
happy hour retirees

a residence gated
with christ's cross
sunflowers
and political flags.

- "a beautiful
place
somewhere far
away "

blood
slowly streaming
a cold, deep grate

the girl
died as she

but born he

killed by them

born not as
but died as such

the killer
armed with
hateful agenda
spread nationwide.

- *" born like it "*

illness
in body
the mind, the spirit, the world

alone with our toys
withering

we learned
in the hardest way

we're all worthless on our own

we listen only to us

and can you be surprised?

this divided house
remains divided
and soon dies
in the same way.

- *" equality in
isolation "*

injustice sells
merch, shirts, and friendly get togethers

coming soon to a city near you

tagline posterboards
songs of peace and love
for a change that...

well, nothing changed.

call now and receive

detesters in cars
psychopaths fond of bricks

destruction and mayhem

just like in the movies

coming soon.

\- *" protest llc "*

the star knows not
of earthling's problems

as they are too far and too high
to ever look down

so it sings its songs

and plays pretend

and those below
fire back

soon, then
the star
becomes an asteroid
and crashes on its face.

- " *imagine* "

a tool for consistency

conversation, news, expression

competition, lies, and theft

the unblinking eye
the unclosed lips

our algorithms shall outlive us

the soul is data

this xanadu penitentiary
we have made for ourselves.

- " the semi-
physical world "

target of the day

someone who we didn't
care to remember

their treason:
disagreement

the punishment thus
beratement of insults and anger
and nothing more

those worse, well
we haven't gotten to yet
but promises, we will.

- *" target of
the day "*

a wide reaching audience
a wide reaching tongue

pardon pardon
please excuse me

get to the front for a question

as they exclaim belligerent falsehoods

where is your evidences?
how indeed do you know?

the barker stands still
as an audience member
grabs me by the throat
and carves me like dinner.

- " barker "

big bad man
walks into a saloon
holds his piece
says a final prayer

his motives many
his head unbounded

the patrons
stood no chance

the brave resistance
stood benign

he has a drink
and runs out the back.

- *" high noon "*

i came to visit a friend this day

they bitched and moaned
as i soiled the front door

the side door, they said
is the only way in

the side door they presented

abundant:
latches and locks
screen doors and passwords

the answer of which
they only knew

what a fool they were
that giant, neon sign
"ENTER HERE"
that person-sized
hole in the fencing
gave way for an extended stay.

- *" the visit "*

in night's dark blanket
when all are asleep
i emerge into
a moth anew

i fly by moonlight
past trees, houses, and streets
looking for cool puddles
a short life to have

until then i found
something so beautiful
words failed to describe
what my eyes had found

so bright so blooming
these wings can't help
closer and closer to this
what i cannot deny

the feeling of warmth
inescapable and ever so desirable
i leave to return
again, and again
one night i found
the light went out
though disappointment inside
there's always more lights around

i don't know what it was
surrounded by other moths
who were just like me
just wanting to survive the night.

- *" moths "*

same heat
different climate

new teeth
different spit

again

same death
different blood

same rage
different machine

and again

same smoke
different fire

and over

same words
different letters

over.

- *" over and over
and over a- "*

book three
'me, you'

people talk to people
i will never
understand
try

seems to be
i'm only good talking to me

the bottomless pit
that surrounds their iris

i worship seclusion
but bend to isolation

i long to those moments
togetherness
just another daydream.

- " attention
attention "

once a friend
now just another
memory in the archive
sometimes i just wanna
bring you out again for old
time's sake
but i know
you're the same without me

don't be mistaken
i'm grateful for our time
everything that's given

two people sharing life
whatever way we could

anywhere you are now,
i hope you the best
and i'll be here wishing.

- " to the many
who shared their
time with me "

then time continued
and I've lived longer than you

and soon you'll be gone longer
than you ever were

the soul of life

left us so soon

childhood ended
before us.

- *" longer still "*

more than this:

church on sundays
kids, family, football

bullshit from work
school, friday wine, overtime

a packed minivan
on the way to practice
on the way to the mall
on the way to somewhere

never more
than this weekly happenings

never more
i see my flawed existence.

- " another
week "

we just met
i know you know

there's just this

i feel it

can't you?
this love?
it's just me i guess

but, i can't deny
it's all for you.

- *" strangelove "*

locals in your area

hundreds of thousands want to fuck

and i do too

to chew those crumbs
to spit that syrup

let's play hangman

you sit and choke
and i do what i want.

- " brothers
don't say
mishmash "

oh, you make me sad,
sickened, afraid

you've really
made things worse

where's the
love and trust you swore?

the red paint appearing
only after your actions

much too late to change
but not too late to break

erasing our love
forced to keep trauma.

- *" pov "*

i know what i did
but let's talk about you

the issue is mine

i hate myself
for the things you do

let me preach my vitriol
and let it sink in your stomach
next to the pills
i'll make myself swallow.

- *"mine, yours,*
and mine "

take a pill
and then ten more

you didn't want me
to interrupt self-destruction

if you wanted me gone so bad...

put the blame on me
then do it again

then do it again

this two way exchange of regret

a match burned at both sides

still ends up swallowing itself.

- " the window
by the sink "

i'm not a bitter guy
'least not anymore
life's too short for this
huffing at theoreticals

we were what was
before today had objected

this i hope you know

health and wellness
despite these times
clarity in your minds
a purpose with your steps

and if someone else you've found

has done what i couldn't

i hope it lasts
and it lasts for life

despite what we weren't.

- *" exes in oh "*

pardon the interruption
i hate to bother
but just a quick word

it's been a while

everything became amuck

but time has passed
and i believe i can
do better than i did

let's go out sometime

have a cup of warm remembrance

for good times gone
and good times to come
and the bullshit day to day

still young for now

for now let's just ride

shoot the shit
rip the bandages
chop the door's boards.

- " *remember me* "

book four
'a reflection'

i live in a hotel
wake up every day in
a room I can't remember
go to sleep at night
in one i've never seen

innkeeper, receptionist, manager
titles for barren business
no one checks in or out
always waiting for a visitor
often, i just stare at the door

some days i wake up
with someone next to me
they tell me good morning
and show me out

other days i wake up
i'm drowning in the indoor pool
no lights or crew to assist
little energy to reach the top
barely reaching for another breath

sometimes i can't sleep
the staring poster on the wall
showing me everything i shouldn't

a remote-less buzzing television
the cacophonous neighbors

i dream someday of locking the door
being somewhere i'm familiar
a room to call my own, finally
no neighbors, or strangers,
posters, pools, or unfamiliar places

it's not up to me
i go down with this hotel
no choice for me to quit
someone's gotta run things
i just don't want it to
bring me down.

- " hotel "

i wanna stay
stay and try
god knows it's all
we can ever do

maybe i've had enough
seen all there is

a silent exit to give

no one notices, gives a glance.

- *" maybe "*

the mirror, a tricky object
it reflects, never displays
as i see myself
i don't see a man
only tangible confusion

known not hopefully for
my contents or how i walk
or what's on paperwork
but, to find happiness with self
a challenge never much expects

the only body i'll have
i want to treat well
find ease with the given

if i had it different, though
i'd hope it'd be easier

in self-expression
in comfort with self
and with emotion
or better knowledge of my ways

or at least,
a guy could dream.

- *" missed "*

...i guess

i never found the best word

just the feeling of it
how i felt

how i'm feeling

never enough

too much, too soon

why am i wanted
but never needed enough?

the past never present
tomorrow just another.

shaking hands with the
thin air
feet floating above

you will never know
how i feel

only the window.

- *" unf "*

to live with closed doors
tinted blinds and sealed windows
eventually; you'll forget how to open up
to stay away doesn't mean you're home

i know when they talk about me
i know when they don't
both are equally terrifying.

- *" noise "*

this is it now

a forward marching inevitable

the point in time now

it's time to choose

and god forbid
when the line you choose
doesn't follow its path

it's on you
it's on you.

- *" ...and*
this is now "

just to have myself
as myself
no one else but me
stretch marks in my psyche

be yourself

bullshit

be others closest to you
pretty pinboard

straight
laced
kempt

fuck more
go out more
live more

talk more
i can only give as
much as i can

i cannot
what you want me

i write, think
too much
but it helps
i'm too young to care
what other mouth-breathers
stare at all day

good lord it gets tiring
not being me,
i'm nothing special

move, ben

you're going to crash.

- " *pride* "

woe in
the season of growth
blemishes on clay

drowning in cesspools
you had to drink it in

nobody really around

i followed my ways
i ate the fruit
it tore me apart
and blew up inside

and you may say
"what happened to dismay?"

i chose the way
of the chain fence
and the barking, foam-mouthed
mutt.

- *" i was a
teenage incel "*

one, three
forward or backward; i cannot tell
each one like the rest
each one their own consciousness

telling me what to do
angels and demons
never telling which one
is which

it's so complicated
the languages they speak

unintelligible

i've heard it all before.

\- *" walking "*

i am paranoid of unlooking gaze

the eyes that haven't looked my way

careless of my existence

i wonder what their

peripherals think

if they notice what i do

the imbalanced curvature of flat feet

and the freckle that my shoes grew.

- *" out in the
open "*

i put the "bet"
in "maybe today"

fold

next time
for sure i know

i put the hex
in "maybe next time, then."

*- " gambler's
fallacy "*

big boy
kind of always been

in a family
of party balloons

we pop often

i'm working to delay it.

- *" lad lard "*

so, here i am now
what's next?

made it this far
just to say i did
what's the purpose
of that?

just another collision
no one will hear
just another mess.

- *" what's
next? "*

my eyes shame
what my fingers do
they're mute

they tell me
what i
shouldn't do

uninterested.

- *" witness "*

there are many ways
hundreds in just one hand
to scratch an itch

it's so heavy – burdening
screams and rattles,
"please, just heed me now
let me out, no more!" it begs

an order only i can bring.

- *" thirst "*

57

i've been feeling it
as it feels me

i've made it worse
as it made me worse

you know i never knew
what a silenced mouth could do
i didn't want to interrupt
i just wanted to listen
i wanted to be a friend

because everyone around me
had it worse than me it seems

so i guess i never really
spoke up before long
i just wanted to listen

what a silenced mouth could do.

- " *listen* "

my sister was born in '04
i didn't become a brother
until i was 18

god help me

things before i've done

selfish

this cain i hold
two hands
endless destructive potential

you and me.

- *"   'o brother   "*

lady, lady
she lays in front of me
untouched by fibre

bathed in silicon and screen

i don't smoke
she leaves me burned
and keeps me awake

she rests
her chokehold on me
and breathes out
her addiction.

- *" primal
insecurity "*

this old street
i saw myself as a child
his face slowly
tearing off
peeling away from adhesive

closed shops

as i got closer to the
end of the street

looking back to see
all that's left

i walked back
everything was the
same, but not entirely.

- *" town "*

in 30 years or 30 seconds
what is learned turns into
what is lived

a face scarred from
taking the punches
will someday
roll with them
like good times.

- " *30 years* "

the worst part of youth
so much time to have
yet more than enough to waste
who knows which is which?

don't plan on living to 25
yet i didn't plan on making it this far
that's life i guess,
i fall under weights of felled plans.

- *" plans "*

book five
'good morning'

always moving forward

unstoppable

unending

realizing what's been
has been for long

the stains on the carpet
turn back into pattern
you never remembered

and as you grow older
the people who've left you
the lost time longer than they've
spent with you

the "would've" is more than you've had

the house creaks behind your ear

and as your threadbare soul
withers into mist
another neighborly smile

all the love you'll never receive
the stale hope you'll forget
and then

another day.

- *" ripple "*

following time
the many, endless footprints
in the sand
never can i catch up – can we catch up
just following the shadow, learning the motion
and hoping that we repeat it well

i like to think i know tomorrow
at least that i'll wake up
but that's not guaranteed
and by the time it's over
what's expected is contradicted

i'm young, they say, but i'm old
as old as i can be
as knowing as i could know
but only i know nothing, just lessons
others have taught me
that they were told they know

for slowly decaying
on another decaying rock
with other decaying beings
i'd say things could be worse
just my thoughts, anyway.

- *" following
time "*

said this before
we've been here before
before i get
in a loop

whatever you say
or think
i do too

it's become
mundane

textbook

plain

circle in the dirt
i keep drawing

it's been this long
you would've thought
it might be different

it's just comfort
escapism
to think of things
better than this.

\- " *vu* "

the chorus of
a closing door

box springs croak

for a moment
take to consideration

sunshine
bleeding
through the dark.

- *" downtime "*

everything sucks
but
it doesn't fully blow

a locked door
can still open up

these old photobooks
have room for more.

- " after "

everybody's gonna die
from my actions

nothing you haven't heard already

a pathetic
never do nothing
never helped me at all

believe what you will

no concern of mine

but what i know
this way of living
doesn't live long at all.

- *" the big*
harrumph "

children, we all
connected to this soul

a duty

but not
the time spent
on the meaningless

as we usually do

as i have done

this time of change.

one of us
all of us

it takes

a nation
to run one

to be one

fall
and rise again

all of us
one of us

it takes

a person
to care for

to be all.

- *" us all "*

years to gain
months to lose

everything
you'll ever want
you can have

if you need it to
when it all goes wrong
so it can bring you joy.

- " everything
you've ever wanted
(and more) "

i know, yes
i know

these faces i know
i only ever saw
because i saw them often

what's lost
can be found
with effort

what's old
can be restored

god knows

i need more than me

to get by sometimes.

- *" like family "*

it's only life
starting and stopping everyday
it's what you make it
jokes need a punchline
and i'll make it sweet

it's only life
and it ends for us all
but don't be mistaken
a life lived in death
is no life lived at all.

\- *" it's only life "*

don't get attached
nothing special sought
bringing in weekly groceries

cleaning out drawers
old receipts and dust bunnies

to work and back

writing down these lines
hoping i find someone
that'll feel better

of me if not

and if you see this
i've made it halfway.

- " *i am* "

show me the dawn's needles
today's vagrancies
yesterday's lessons
buried in the tongue

show me
the door to your room
show me around
tell me about your days
and the one you had recently

show me
what i've done wrong
and congratulate my failures
shout at the cut corners
the ways i make time pass

show me
how to dance in tunnel light
the night comes soon
and how to
fall in love with the moon

show me
before i leave

how to just make be
and never
too much.

- *" show me "*

i'll be honest

i'm bad at it

these days keep passing
and i learn
i've barely known myself
the things we do

i try

i'm bad at it

honesty as a window
into an endless sea
i finally learned to swim

i've always been someone
just never known it
until i took myself
around
and saw what i have

despite what i've had
it shows its claws
the cuts never made
that deep

someday i'll learn

but not today

someday i'll know

not soon

but since i'm still on
this side of the dirt
i'm gonna use it
to make more flowers
and bloom

day for day
night to night
i'm glad i'm here
i'm happy for life

things may be rough
but

hell, it's always been so

try as we must
as you must

just never dig mudholes
just to give yourself
something to fill

speaking of yesterday
i hope today can be better

the worse that i fear

the farther it's behind

and now and then
i look to back then
what bothered me most
doesn't bother me now
fortunately fortunate

i've learned what i needed

sometimes harder than usual

but a lesson learned
is better than one
forgotten

till death do we part

set in our ways

in my own way

in the end

there's only one of me
talking to
an army of you

gladly.

- *" always "*

9 798884 595592